TAKING ON
THE PLASTICS
CRISIS

HANNAH TESTA

PENGUIN WORKSHOP

**I'd like to dedicate this book to my parents
and my family and friends for their endless
love and support—HT**

PENGUIN WORKSHOP
An Imprint of Penguin Random House LLC, New York

Text copyright © 2020 by Hannah Testa. Illustrations copyright © 2020 by
Penguin Random House LLC. All rights reserved. Published by Penguin Workshop,
an imprint of Penguin Random House LLC, New York. PENGUIN and
PENGUIN WORKSHOP are trademarks of Penguin Books Ltd, and the W colophon
is a registered trademark of Penguin Random House LLC. Manufactured in China.

Visit us online at www.penguinrandomhouse.com.

Library of Congress Cataloging-in-Publication Data is available upon request.

ISBN 9780593223338   10 9 8 7 6 5 4 3 2 1

PROLOGUE

February 15, 2018: It might seem like an ordinary, forgettable date, but in the state of Georgia, it was Plastic Pollution Awareness Day—a day I helped create with a state senator when I was fourteen.

I remember that day like it was yesterday. I stood inside the Georgia State Capitol, holding a rolled-up paper in my clammy hands. My heart was fluttering. My fingers trembled with fear. I was about to deliver a speech to fifty-six state senators. But first I had to wait for the speaker—an adult—at the podium to finish hers.

From the side of the stage, I gazed out at the crowd: No one seemed to be paying any attention to the person giving her speech. My chest tightened.

I had been working toward this moment for a year—to be on this very stage to raise awareness about the growing plastics crisis. And all I could think was how no one would listen to my speech either, especially because I was just a teenager.

Over the course of 2017, I started to see the plastics industry for what it really was: powerful corporations and lobbyists, people paid by companies to influence politicians. And the last thing they wanted was for a speech like mine to be heard. In fact, the plastics industry came out in full force to stop this event from happening, and when I really think about it, their motives can be summed up with one word: *fear*.

Fear that I might shine a light on the realities of single-use plastics and their negative impact on the environment, animal welfare, and our health. Fear that the industry would lose money, as it saw a decline in the use of plastic. Fear that people like me were using their voices. But any attempts to stop me only made me want to speak louder. So, I stood my ground.

But as I stood in the capitol building, ready

to deliver that speech, I suddenly started to lose confidence in myself. If the senators weren't listening to an adult, why would they listen to me?

Each passing minute felt longer than the next. As the woman at the podium spoke her last words into the microphone, the state senators hardly seemed to notice. No one clapped. *Tough crowd*, I thought. I took a deep breath. It was my turn. I felt my legs quiver as I stepped up to the podium and lowered the microphone. I looked out at the room, scattered with senators milling about, talking among themselves, paying little attention to me. I scanned the audience and found my mom and brother smiling at me. Beside me stood my dad, and my friend and mentor, John R. Seydel, a director with the city of Atlanta. On my other side was Senator Nan Orrock, the politician I worked with to create this historic day. For a brief moment, I felt at ease, having all these people with me for support.

I took another deep breath to soak in this moment: There I was, a high-school freshman who wasn't even of voting age, and yet I was about to deliver a speech to the decision makers in my home state of Georgia. Forget "pinch me" moments—this was make-or-break.

I opened my mouth and began my speech. Suddenly, it was as if every senator simultaneously realized that there was a teenager at the mic. Silence blanketed the room and every eye was on me. Everyone was listening to me. To my voice.

For the next few minutes, I spoke about the growing crisis before us. I spoke about how plastic is washing up on our shores by the ton—flooding our oceans and choking our animal and marine life. And how microplastics are seeping into our bodies through water bottles and other single-use plastics. And how, by 2050, plastic production is projected to quadruple, further adding to carbon dioxide emissions that contribute to climate change—unless we act *now*.

"This is our moment. This is our movement. This is our mission," I said, wrapping up my speech. I concluded it with a final question: "Are you with us?"

My speech was met with an overwhelming round of applause.

From that moment—that unforgettable February

day—I recognized firsthand that young people have voices, and we *can* be heard. I realized then and there that political movements start with a decision to use our voices. And for me, it started with the decision to take on the plastics crisis.

On my second birthday, my parents drove from our home in Baltimore, Maryland, to Jacksonville, Florida, so I could see the beach for the very first time. I've been fascinated by all things aquatic for as long as I can remember. In my mind, this blue underworld was pristine. It was filled with majestic sea creatures and unknowns that I so desperately wanted to discover. I couldn't get enough.

When we arrived at the beach, I was in awe. I took it all in: the way a handful of sand would dance its way around and through my fingers; the way the waves crashed upon the shore; the way the ocean air smelled so crisp and clean. Even though I was nearly a thousand miles from Baltimore, I found a second home. From that moment on, I felt a connection to nature.

When I was five, our family moved from Baltimore to Atlanta, Georgia. We were just one small family but we tried to do our part to take care of the planet through sustainable practices. We carried reusable bags to the grocery store. We picked up litter. We conserved water and electricity wherever possible. And, of course, we recycled.

In Atlanta, I spent my childhood playing in the woods, taking walks on nature trails with my family, and helping to take care of the garden we grew in our backyard. It was in that garden where my parents taught me to respect nature and all its creatures. It felt like a small miracle—the idea that you can plant a seed in the earth and with some water, sunlight, and time, you'll have a vegetable you can eat.

When I was in kindergarten, I remember asking my mom if I could give tomato plants to all my classmates. All twenty-five of them. My mother was hesitant. She knew that buying that many tomato plants would be expensive. So, she bought me a pack of seeds instead. My mom told me that if I took care of the plants for the next few months, I could give them to my classmates on Earth Day. Like most parents of young children, they figured I would forget about the plants in a few days and be on to my next obsession.

But for the next eight weeks, I rushed home after school to water the tomato plants. My parents couldn't believe my commitment. When Earth Day came around, I led a show-and-tell about why we celebrate Earth Day every year. I ended my short presentation by handing each of my classmates a tomato plant that I had grown for them.

As I grew older, I loved learning more and more about our planet and all its animals.

But when I was ten years old, my mom showed me a video of rhinos in South Africa being killed for sport and poached for their horns, which could be sold for money. A single horn could fetch more money per kilogram than gold. In the video, I witnessed the poachers' practices. First, they shot the rhino with a very strong tranquilizer gun to bring the animal down. Then, the poacher hacked the horn off the rhino while it was unconscious, leaving the rhino bloody and left for dead.

I was in shock.

I couldn't comprehend why this barbaric ritual was happening in the first place, and why no one was putting a stop to this cruel practice.

Images from that video haunted me for the next few weeks. Once my eyes were opened, I couldn't stop watching more videos and reading articles online. In one video, I learned how elephants were being killed for their ivory. In another, I saw how every year, dolphins, whales, and porpoises were being slaughtered by the thousands in Japan. Then I read an article about explorer Robert Swan, the first person to walk to both the North and South Poles. Swan dedicated his life's work to the preservation of Antarctica. He wrote, "The greatest threat to our planet is the belief that someone else will save it."

He was right. I was only ten, but I knew that I could no longer simply sit idly in my home as an observer. I needed to act; the question was how. So, I told my mom I wanted to do something. But she was reluctant.

I remember her saying, "What can *we* do about it?"

I wasn't satisfied with that answer. I knew that there must be *something* I could do. So, I went back online and learned about an organization that was collecting petitions that would ultimately be hand delivered to the president of South Africa to influence the government to stop the practice of poaching rhinos for their horns. To support their cause, I committed to collecting five hundred signatures for the petition. I asked my mom if she could help, but again, she was hesitant.

She said that we didn't even know fifty people, so how would we collect five hundred signatures? Still, she could see the look on my face and knew how eager I was to contribute to this cause. So, she agreed, not knowing exactly how we would collect so many signatures. (Years later, my mom would tell me she had envisioned a lit candle in me and didn't want to extinguish that flame by saying no.)

So, when I had an idea to invite people to our house to sign the petition and spread the word to their friends, neighbors, and families, my mom couldn't say no. After forty-eight hours, we had close to two hundred signatures. A few weeks later, after talking to lots of people in our community, I had reached my goal. But not wanting to stop at five hundred, I continued my work and ended up with well over two thousand signatures.

But when I sent in those two thousand signatures, it was a bittersweet moment: I had achieved what I had set out to do, but it was over—just like that. I wanted to do more. Now that I had a taste for creating change, I was eager for another challenge.

When my mom told me about a fundraiser event happening at a local horse-rescue farm, I found my next opportunity. I was particularly interested in attending because I loved horses. So, with my parents, my brother, and one of my friends, we drove to the farm to see all the horses. In my head, I pictured these beautiful animals roaming free on the land with the wind in their manes. When we arrived, it was anything but that majestic picture I had envisioned. Everything there was old and run-down: the stables, the troughs, and even the horses.

At the farm, we met a volunteer who showed us around the property. She explained how the average cost to run the farm each month was $10,000 and how all their funds were collected from donations. She explained how the farm sometimes couldn't reach its $10,000 minimum, and this was why the farm was in its state of disrepair. When we entered the horse stables, she told us stories of the different horses and why they were there: Some had been hit by cars, others dragged behind tractors, and some were simply abandoned to starve.

Each horse had a story worse than the last. My heart hurt just thinking of all the horrific things these beautiful creatures had to endure. On the drive home, I knew I had to do something for them.

That night, I explained the conditions of the farm to some friends. I suggested we do a fundraiser. At the time, I was only ten years old, and like most kids my age, my friends and I loved American Girl dolls. Coincidentally, the American "Girl of the Year" was Saige, who was a young girl with a horse. There was even a movie about Saige and her horse, called *American Girl: Saige Paints the Sky*. So, we thought it would be a good idea to do a movie night at the farm and show the movie to raise funds for it. Plus, the movie would be perfect for kids who love dolls and horses. For the next few months, my friends and I prepared. We all gave ourselves different roles at the fundraiser: One would work concessions, one would collect the entrance fees, and others would lead people on a tour of the rescue farm.

About three hundred people visited the farm, and with the admission fee and money for food, drinks, and various raffles, we raised about $2,400. CBS 46 Atlanta featured the event that night and the following morning, and after a local viewer saw the story on the news, they wrote a check for $10,000 for the organization. (My parents still tear up when they watch the video online.)

From the success of this one event that we coordinated, my ambitions grew farther, wider. Through my initial advocacy work with animals, I began to learn more about plastic pollution because of its impact on them. But it wasn't until I watched the documentary *Plastic Paradise* that I really grasped the severity of this crisis.

In the documentary, Angela Sun, an American journalist and documentary filmmaker, travels to the Midway Islands, an atoll off the coast of Hawaii, to witness firsthand the impact of plastic pollution on humans and animals. Midway is home to a tiny former US naval base in the middle of the Pacific Ocean, two thousand miles from the nearest continent and about halfway between North America and Asia. Yet, in the documentary, Sun shows how literally tons of plastic are washing up on the atoll's shore, despite it being thousands of miles from where the plastic originated. I learned that plastic items in the continental United States—a water bottle, a plastic bag, or even a single-use plastic cup—can end up on the shores of faraway islands. And what's worse is that this plastic finds its way into the bellies of animals and marine life, like the iconic albatross.

The albatross, which are already endangered birds, flock to these islands by the millions. But when they arrive, they often mistake the plastic for food.

In Sun's documentary, Midway looks like a postwar battlefield, with dead birds scattered everywhere. She explains that scientists report more than 97 percent of these dead albatross chicks and more than 89 percent of dead adult birds on this island contained plastic in their stomachs.

To prove her point even further, Sun performs a simple blood test on herself to show how BPA—Bisphenol A, a chemical found in some plastics—has made its way into her bloodstream in a matter of minutes after holding plastic that had washed up on the shore. But the most troubling part was learning how the plastics industry has been trying to cover up the problem.

I felt like my head was buried in the sand. I realized that, like most people, I never gave much thought to all the plastic we use and then discard daily. And I never thought about how it all permeates every corner of the planet, ending up in landfills and in our streets, parks, rivers, and oceans. I realized that our individual actions and habits have such a large-scale impact on the world. I wanted to do more to help.

Initially, I turned to the Plastic Pollution Coalition—a nonprofit dedicated to educating the public on plastic pollution—for information and to help get me on my way.

Soon enough I wanted to forge my own path.

So, what started as a small Facebook page would, in just a few years, evolve into a fully organized nonprofit: Hannah4Change.org. I had my mission and work cut out for me.

But first, I knew I had to learn everything I could about plastic.

In many ways, plastic can be considered a miracle product. Plastic has the power to help save lives in the form of prosthetics and heart valves. By swapping out steel for plastic, we are able to manufacture more fuel-efficient cars, quickly and at a more affordable price for consumers. Without plastic, we would have never put a man on the moon by 1969. Plastic, it can be argued, has changed the world for the better.

But too much of anything can be a problem. Plastic has managed to seep into nearly every facet of our modern lives, so much so that it's hard to imagine a world *without* plastic. In developed countries like the United States, where the majority of the population doesn't think twice about throwing away something used only once, the problem is made even worse. Most people are willing to ignore the consequences of single-use plastics—such as bottles, bags, and cups—because they offer us a quick convenience, like being able to take coffee or a sandwich on the go.

Our consumer habits continue to add to our global dependency on plastic. It seems like there is no escape. It's everywhere. It's under our sinks: shampoos and conditioners and toothbrushes, to name a few. It's in our pantries, our refrigerators, and our freezers. Most of the food we buy is wrapped in plastic packaging. Our kitchen cabinets are riddled with plastic cups, plates, and bags. Tucked away in our closets and bedrooms are clothes and linens, most of which are made from plastic.

And now some studies are finding plastic in rain, arctic snow, the air we breathe, and, according to the Medical University of Vienna in Austria, in tap water, bottled water, and even our own feces. Yes, that means we are unknowingly consuming and ingesting plastic.

Despite our heavy reliance on plastic, it hasn't been around for very long. Plastic was first invented in 1907.

But it wasn't until the breakout of the Second World War in 1939 that plastic became vital for the war effort, to help make parts for planes and tires for vehicles. The product's value was quickly recognized by governments for its many uses and low manufacturing costs. After the war, plastic made its way from the front lines into our households as companies, too, recognized its value to create convenient, single-use products and at a much lower cost. Since then, plastic production has continued to grow astronomically: 300 million tons of plastic are produced each year around the globe, which is nearly equivalent to the weight of the entire human population.

What's even more troubling is that almost half of that production is designed to be used just once, and then thrown away. And even though we don't see it once it's disposed, it's never really gone. Humans have filled the planet with plastics that don't degrade. And while plastic has made our lives convenient in many aspects, that convenience comes with a steep price: the potential to destroy our planet.

Plastic begins in the ground as crude oil, a precious and valuable fossil fuel. This oil is pumped out of the ground and into refineries to be mixed with chemical additives (phthalates and bisphenols) and then turned into plastic pellets called nurdles. The nurdles are transported to manufacturing plants where they are heated and molded into desired shapes. These plastic products are then shipped, bought, used, and discarded. Although it takes several months to produce single-use plastics, and they are created by fossil fuels that have been underground for centuries, we use them in many cases for just a few minutes.

Plastic is designed to be durable and long lasting, which is great for some applications, but for items that we use for such a temporary time, this creates an enormous problem.

Plastic is so durable that it doesn't break down or biodegrade but instead breaks up into smaller and smaller pieces. These pieces can take centuries to fully degrade and disappear. This means that virtually every single piece of plastic that has ever been made still exists on our planet somewhere (unless it's been incinerated, which releases particle pollution). Think about that: Something we often use just once, like a plastic bag or cup, will remain on our earth for hundreds or even thousands of years!

As the world's population continues to grow, so does the demand for plastic. Plastic production across the globe has spiraled out of control, and despite some efforts to become more environmentally conscious, plastic production continues to rise. Most reputable studies project that by 2050, plastic production will increase by four times. Unless we take action now, scientists predict that around the same time, the plastic in the ocean will outweigh the fish!

No matter how far you live from the nearest ocean, the plastic you discard can easily end up there. Our sewers, streams, and rivers act as a superhighway for your plastic bottle to travel hundreds of miles away and into the ocean. And because plastic is lightweight, it can easily go anywhere the wind can take it. Everywhere it goes, the toxins from the plastic leach into the environment. This can lead to a number of concerns.

While trees provide us with some oxygen, most of the oxygen we breathe is actually produced from marine life in the ocean. Approximately every other breath we take is generated from the ocean. Today, our oceans are suffering, partly due to all the trash that ends up there. Roughly eight million metric tons of plastic make their way into the ocean each year, which is equivalent to five grocery bags filled with plastic for every foot of coastline in the world.

The ocean is also suffering due to hazardous chemicals from the plastic debris. Plastic debris uses up oxygen as it degrades, resulting in low levels of oxygen in the water. Decreasing oxygen levels affect the survival of marine life, including whales, dolphins, and penguins—but also humans, since we rely on the ocean for oxygen.

Another factor at play here is gyres. A gyre is basically a system of ocean currents, and there is one in every major ocean. These oceanic currents pull trash toward the center—like a large whirlpool—and trap it there, creating a garbage vortex of what looks like cloudy, plastic smog. The gyre in the North Pacific Ocean has created the most "famous" (if you can call it that) accumulation of ocean plastic in the world, commonly called the Great Pacific Garbage Patch. This large region in the North Pacific Ocean contains high concentrations of plastic, much of which is tiny and below the surface.

Large concentrations of plastic in the ocean lead to it being ingested by marine life. As smaller marine life eat the plastic, they pass it up the food chain as bigger sea creatures eat them. Once humans eat seafood (and drink water), plastic enters our systems and ultimately ends up in our feces. Recent studies state that we eat about five grams of plastic every week—that's a spoonful of plastic! Or, to put it in even more disgusting terms, in a single year the average human ingests 250 grams of plastic. That's like eating a heaping plate full of plastic. This is just one of the reasons I don't eat seafood.

What's worse is that chemicals leached by plastic are in the blood and tissue of nearly all humans alive today. Various studies link exposure to these chemicals to cancers, birth defects, impaired immunity, hormone disruption, and other ailments.

Plastic also releases toxins into the food and drinks it comes in contact with. So, yes, your plastic coffee cup is leaching toxins into your coffee. It's no surprise that plastic is considered a potentially human carcinogenic material. (This is just a fancy way to say that it may be linked to cancer).

Some chemicals in plastic, such as BPA, have been called out by scientists as they may put children's health at risk, but there are plenty of other chemicals in plastic that we just don't have sufficient information on. Still, it's enough information to be a cause of great concern.

Plastic is also a problem for communities that rely on beaches and waterways for tourism and food, like the island of Mauritius in the Indian Ocean, the birthplace of my mother's parents. I have been fortunate enough to visit many beaches and coastal communities across the world, and I am just shocked at the amount of plastic that I find.

In early 2019 while on a visit to Brunei, a country in Asia that is mostly rainforest, I was able to visit a beautiful landmark called Kampong Ayer, a six-hundred-year-old water village built on stilts where over 13,000 residents live. There, I saw large amounts of garbage floating on the river beneath the community. Many of the residents tossed trash into the river because the tide would take it away. But when the tide came and went, a lot of trash remained, much of it plastic. And while the sight of it was mortifying, I learned that the people living in the village relied on the fish in that water as their primary food source. People were eating the fish that was eating their trash, but they still failed to make the connection that they were ingesting their own garbage.

It's clear that our reliance on plastic is a serious concern for our planet and that reducing plastic pollution is truly an urgent global matter. Still, there's a lot we need to do to help reduce our plastic consumption.

Most people probably think that because they recycle, they are doing everything they can to fight plastic pollution. But it turns out that recycling isn't the perfect solution we have been led to believe. The system is broken. And no, I'm not suggesting that we stop recycling, because we shouldn't. It's just that recycling alone isn't really enough. Unfortunately, if we're not recycling properly, we may be causing more of a problem.

The great recycling myth we've all been led to believe—that recycling is the answer—has lulled us into nearly guilt-free consumption of plastic products. This is a result of shrewd marketing by the plastics industry. Their marketing has also given us the false expectation that any plastic we buy that includes the recycling symbol (the green triangle with the number inside) can be recycled without implications. This is far from the truth. There are lots of issues and challenges for consumers and communities when it comes to recycling.

First and foremost, the recycling symbol we see on many plastic products doesn't mean the product is necessarily able to be recycled; it merely identifies the type of plastic material. Logos with the numerals 1 or 2, for example, are very common types of plastic, yet numerals 3 through 7 are less common. Many people think that if they see the symbol, it means "I can recycle this," but that isn't always the case.

Second, recycling isn't easy. It takes effort for individuals and consumers to separate plastic for recycling from the regular trash. For instance, when dining at a fast-food restaurant that has recycling bins, there's a good chance of seeing diners throwing away all of their trash without taking the time to separate the recycling from the regular trash. This all-too-regular occurrence is just a part of the reason why less than 10 percent of the world's plastic gets recycled (and that percentage appears to be declining year after year).

Third, recycling is confusing and isn't very straightforward. What can be recycled? What cannot be recycled? Can we recycle plastic bags? Do we have to clean the plastic material before recycling? What about the labels and caps on bottles? Are there some plastics that cannot be recycled? These are just a handful of the many questions that plague the most-conscious consumers, who are trying to do their part to help the planet.

Unfortunately, there aren't any easy answers to these questions—as it usually depends on the policies of your local jurisdiction. What's worse, these policies may change over time, causing even more confusion. For example, my local county recently stopped accepting glass in curbside recycling pickup, so my family and I did research and found other options. Now we collect our household glass and take it to a local recycling center ourselves. Yet I still see people discarding glass with their plastic for curbside recycling. Imagine how hard it must be for county workers to separate the glass from the plastic at the recycling center.

What's most upsetting is that a majority of the plastic in recycling bins doesn't end up getting recycled after all; it actually ends up in the landfill or incinerated. This is due to several reasons: Sometimes the plastic is contaminated with food particles or other items that got mixed in with the plastic and can't be easily cleaned or sorted, so they are put into the regular trash and sent to the landfill. And for some plastic products, such as straws, utensils, and Styrofoam products, there isn't a practical way for them to be recycled.

Recycling also relies on supply and demand, meaning that once plastic arrives at the recycling center and is sorted into different categories based on type of material, will there be a buyer for it? If there is no buyer for these plastics to produce new products, the recycling center has no choice but to discard the plastics into the landfill or incinerator. All that hard work for nothing! In fact, entire categories of plastic are rarely recycled. And if they are, they are mostly down cycled, which is when plastic is recycled into a lower-quality of plastic that makes it harder to recycle down the line. Of the seven types of plastics that consumers put into their recycling bins, five categories are typically not recycled due to lack of demand and the high costs to recycle them.

In other words, while the average citizen doesn't see it or realize it, behind the scenes, the concept of recycling has led us to believe that everything we put into the recycling bin gets turned into something new, when, in fact, much of it is thrown away. The bottom line is that recycling is not the solution we should rely on to solve the plastic pollution crisis.

To complicate this further, the majority of our plastic that is earmarked for recycling centers actually gets shipped overseas, an "out of sight, out of mind" approach by nations such as the United States. Many developed countries have been sending the vast majority of their plastic to China for years, but in 2017, China decided to refuse most of the world's plastic. Other countries have agreed to take some of our plastic (and some of those countries later decided to stop this practice), but it is believed that their waste-management practices are not as strict as those in the United States. As a result, these materials end up being burned or dumped into the environment. This shift in policies—countries refusing the waste from the United States—has made it very difficult for American cities and towns, and hundreds have canceled or reduced their recycling programs.

Recycling is also expensive for communities and local governments. Some of our tax dollars help our local cities and towns recycle. Recycling requires equipment and employees to pick up, sort, and discard these materials. If we all used less plastic in the first place, our tax dollars—that would otherwise have been used for recycling—could be distributed elsewhere.

So what can we do if recycling is so broken? To make our recycling systems work effectively, we need our federal, state, and local governments to make recycling easier, with clear and consistent guidelines and more incentives to encourage greater participation. In fact, at the time of this writing, I was one of a handful of eco-activists who spoke in support of a federal bill being considered in Washington, DC, called the Break Free From Plastic Pollution Act. Being the youngest person at the introduction of this comprehensive bill, I was honored to be a part of this huge event. If we can get this bill to pass, it will require producers of packaging, containers, and food-service products to design, manage, and finance waste and recycling programs; ban certain single-use plastic products that are not recyclable; and place a fee on carryout bags.

We also need companies to make 100 percent of their packaging recyclable, using 100 percent recycled materials. Better yet, we really need to encourage companies to avoid using plastic in their packaging, and we consumers need to stop buying products with excessive plastic packaging. We need to make companies responsible for the life and end use of their product. We should all work to encourage governments to create policies and incentives that support these sustainable behaviors. And as consumers, the best solution is to refuse plastic, as fewer plastic products used means less plastic going to recycling centers in the first place.

Plastic isn't only a waste problem; it's also a major contributor to climate change. Every stage of plastic's life cycle—from extraction to production to transportation to waste disposal—causes emissions that are a direct cause of climate change. Plastic is made from fossil fuels, and to extract fossil fuels from the ground, a method called fracking is used. But fracking produces methane, an extremely harmful greenhouse gas. The production process itself also releases a lot of carbon dioxide into the atmosphere. In fact, greenhouse gases from plastic production alone are equivalent to almost two hundred coal-fired power plants. To make matters even worse, there are also emissions from transporting plastic products to stores, then into our homes, and ultimately to waste facilities. At the risk of sounding like an alarmist, I mean it when I say the *entire* life cycle of plastic releases greenhouse gas emissions that directly and negatively impact the world's radical change in climate and health at each phase. In short, if you want to lower your carbon footprint, simply refusing single-use plastics is a great start.

What's more, the plastics industry consumes about 5 percent of the world's oil production today, and by 2050 it is projected to consume 20 percent. So, let's get this straight: This precious commodity (oil), which nations already fight over, is being used to make plastic.

Looking beyond the climate crisis, plastic pollution is an issue we all contribute to, but many people like to point fingers when it comes to fixing the problem. Yet plastic doesn't see borders. A plastic package could be made in the United States and might be found in Indonesia, or vice versa. During my beach cleanups, I have seen plastic on the beautiful beaches of Bermuda, Greece, and Jamaica, to name a few, yet much of the plastic came from another region of the world. The sad thing is, many coastal communities rely on the water for ecotourism and seafood, but their economies and ways of life are at risk even though many of these communities use significantly less plastic than other parts of the world.

As an example, Honolulu, Hawaii, now has a law that bans single-use plastics, which is great. Yet the irony is that plastic will still end up on their shores because of how easily plastic travels via ocean gyres. Despite Hawaiians' best legislative efforts, trash will still end up on their coastlines.

And what about the animals in the ocean? They, too, are negatively impacted. Scientists estimate that over a million animals die each year due to ingesting or becoming entangled in plastic. Like the albatross on the Midway Islands, many animals mistake the plastic pieces for food, and the plastic sits in their stomachs and makes them feel full. In a way, plastic is causing animals to starve to death. This breaks my heart, as I have always loved animals and feel they have a right to peaceful lives on this planet.

Whenever I give a speech on the plastics crisis, I like to use this analogy to illustrate my point about refusing plastic. I ask my audience to imagine there is an overflowing tap and water is spilling everywhere.

"What is your first reaction?" I ask them. "You don't grab a mop to first clean the mess. You run to turn off the tap."

We need to do the same with plastic pollution. While beach cleanups are necessary, and recycling properly is important, we cannot rely solely on these solutions to fix our pollution problem. Instead, we need to focus on stopping plastic at the source—and that starts with us, because if we stop buying products made with plastic, businesses will stop producing it.

Fundamentally, we need to alter our relationship with plastic. We have been taught from a young age that the solution to our problem is to follow the three Rs: *reduce*, *reuse*, and *recycle*. But there are two more Rs that are critically important and shouldn't be overlooked: *refuse* and *raise awareness*.

Here are some simple solutions to live a life free of single-use plastics:

Instead of using plastic bags, take reusable bags into the store.

Plastic bags are lightweight and easily get caught in the wind, where they eventually end up on trees, by the side of the road, and in waterways. They are commonly not recycled in curbside recycling programs because they clog the machinery. In the ocean, plastic bags are easily mistaken for jellyfish and eaten by sea turtles. Plastic bags are so common, studies state that the average American uses about five hundred plastic bags per year!

Swap out plastic straws for sustainable ones.

Plastic straws cannot be recycled, and their small size makes it easy for them to find their way into the ocean. And they are a very widely used product—approximately 500 million straws are used daily in the United States alone! That is equivalent to more than 125 school buses filled with straws each day. At restaurants, simply refuse a straw or ask the waiter for alternatives, such as paper, glass, or steel straws, if available.

Use reusable bottles or cups when on the go.

Plastic bottles and cups are major polluters in the ocean, and as a double whammy, the plastic can leach chemicals into the drinks they come in contact with. Globally, over one million plastic drinking bottles are purchased every minute. Also consider water in box cartons, made from recycled paper.

Use metal or bamboo utensils.

Plastic utensils can easily puncture trash bags and end up in the ocean. More than 100 million plastic utensils are used by Americans every day. They can take up to one thousand years to decompose, leaking harmful substances into the earth while they are breaking up. I keep metal utensils in my car and have a pack of reusable bamboo utensils in my backpack.

Seek out reusable containers for food.

Plastic food wrap and sandwich bags can easily add up for a family of four like mine, especially when using them every day to pack lunch for work or school. Use butcher, waxed, or parchment paper. Also, beeswax wraps and reusable pouches are great alternatives for storing food and can be cleaned to use again and again.

Create beauty products from simple ingredients at home.

Cosmetics and beauty products use a lot of unnecessary plastic packaging. There are a few sustainable alternatives that use hardly any plastic packaging for their products.

Shop at secondhand stores to reduce
the amount of new clothes that are made.

And check labels: Most clothes contain plastic microfibers. Avoid polyester, nylon, and polypropylene, and try to buy clothes made from 100 percent cotton.

In addition to these practical solutions,
there are plenty of other ways to reduce
our plastic footprints.

Buy in bulk. Use reusable products whenever possible. Participate in community cleanups. Seek out products that have either no plastic packaging or a small amount of plastic. Support eco-friendly businesses. Join or support one of the hundreds of organizations that are dedicated to the fight against plastic pollution. (I found this to be very effective, as it helped me realize that I wasn't alone and that there were smart people who could provide me with facts and research.)

We all know the 3 Rs: *reduce*, *reuse*, and *recycle*. In my mind, there is a reason recycling is the last R, because it is a last-resort solution and should be viewed that way. When recycling, it's important to adhere to local community rules. To learn what these guidelines are, contact local recycling authorities and find out. They'll be more than happy to help.

Local cleanups are another effective way to remove plastic. And it's easy to participate in one. Cleanups also serve as a great way to educate citizens about how much plastic ends up on local coastlines and other areas. Due to the sheer volume of plastic that enters the ocean, we won't be able to solve this problem by conducting organized cleanups alone, but when I visit a beach, I always try to spend some time picking up trash.

In 2019, I took a trip to Hawaii, a place known for its beautiful beaches. I was invited by my twelve-year-old friend and environmentalist Robbie Bond, who founded the organization Kids Speak for Parks when he was nine. For the last three years, Robbie has been educating people on plastic pollution in addition to teaching others about the beauty of our national parks. Unfortunately, because of Hawaii's geographic location in the Pacific Ocean, parts of the island are where ocean gyres deposit some of the world's trash. Together with other volunteers, we collected five hundred pounds of plastic on Kahuku Beach, and Robbie and I made a 360-degree virtual reality video of our beach cleanup that is being shown in schools to educate students on plastic pollution.

Cleanups don't have to be just on the beaches, either. We can all learn a lot from Lilly Platt from the Netherlands, whose journey started in 2015 when she was walking with her grandfather and noticed a lot of garbage on the street. During their ten-to-fifteen-minute walk, they collected ninety-one pieces of trash. She decided from that moment on that she would always do her best to pick up plastic and keep it out of the environment. When she was just seven, Lilly founded the organization Lilly's Plastic Pickup and, to this day, conducts pickups across the world. She also takes photographs and posts them on social media to spread awareness about the trash she is finding. So far, she has picked up over one hundred thousand pieces of plastic and litter and has made it her mission to inform as many people as possible about plastic pollution.

Lilly's story is a reminder that there is plenty one person can do for the earth. Still, because this is such a monumental challenge, it won't be solved by personal commitment alone. It will also take concerned citizens speaking up to big businesses and holding them accountable.

As a great example of this, I was proud to have worked with a coalition of approximately twenty organizations to collect nearly one million petitions to convince Starbucks to eliminate their plastic-lined paper coffee cups. Due to this pressure, Starbucks pledged $10 million to develop a sustainable coffee cup. Just think, a handful of organizations—including my nonprofit organization—were able to convince such a big business to change its ways. It's important to remember that as consumers, we have a tremendous amount of power. Businesses rely on consumers to buy their products, so if customers decide to no longer buy their products until they ditch their single-use plastics and eliminate their plastic packaging, businesses will shift to match the needs of their customers.

Shelby O'Neil is another eco rock star who also influenced businesses to cut down on their plastic waste. When she was a high-school student in San Juan Bautista, California, her Girl Scout project evolved into the global campaign "No Straw November." Shelby created the event to educate others on the impact of plastic straws, and she also encouraged citizens to count how many straws they were able to eliminate during the month. In 2017, Shelby used her personal power to write to the CEO of Alaska Airlines, and her letter inspired the company to discontinue the use of plastic straws on flights and as well at their airport lounges. She also started the nonprofit Jr Ocean Guardians to continue her work and educate youth on how they can help create a better world.

Based on Shelby's success, I decided to write to American Airlines. After just a few short months, they announced they were phasing out single-use plastics on their flights. The CEO wrote to me to say that while their initiative was underway before my letter, my letter helped spur them to act more quickly.

Saanya Bhargava is another influential eco-activist we can all strive to be like. She was a high-school student in Texas and an intern at Dell when she started to really understand the issue of plastic pollution and became fascinated by science. At fifteen, she inspired Dell to create the Ocean Plastics program, where the goal was to use 100 percent recycled plastic for their packaging, of which 25 percent comes from the ocean. (As of this writing, Dell has reach 94 percent sustainable packaging.) She founded the organization impact.gravitas, which is dedicated to bringing awareness to plastic pollution. She is now a college student at Rice University and continues her activism on campus.

If approaching businesses about reducing their plastic consumption seems daunting, why not start with your school? Chloe-Mei Espinosa has had a passion for the ocean from a young age. As a scuba diver, she directly sees the plastic in our oceans and the impact it is having. At the age of eleven, her dad showed her the viral video of a sea turtle in Costa Rica with a straw stuck in its nose, and it was a wake-up call for her to take action (thank goodness for this powerful video, created by Christine Figgener, as it has impacted a lot of people). Chloe-Mei created the campaign Skip the Plastic Straw to educate people on the harmful effects of plastic straws. So far, she has convinced over a thousand people to sign her pledge to commit to not using plastic straws. In 2018, she convinced the nutrition director of her school district to no longer use straws in any of the thirty-two schools. And that was just the beginning. Now, at just thirteen years old, she has convinced over 128 schools, two hospitals, and a campus to phase out single-use plastic straws.

Chloe-Mei is a prime example of the power we all have by simply signing a petition, sending a letter or email, posting a video on social media, scheduling a meeting with a business or school leader, or joining a protest to influence businesses to switch to sustainable solutions. You can also encourage other consumers to back businesses that are on the journey to sustainability. I have worked closely with a few global brands and companies that are eco-friendly and "putting people before profits," and I like to encourage consumers to support companies that are moving in the right direction to support our earth.

I also like to approach restaurant owners and managers and talk to them about their plastic usage. An easy target to discuss initially is their use of plastic straws. Restaurants can save money by switching to paper straws and only giving out straws upon request (rather than what most restaurants do—handing out plastic straws automatically to all customers). Over the years, I've convinced a few restaurants to switch to paper straws, and I try to support and promote these restaurants whenever possible.

Imagine how much of an impact we can have if we all convince just one business to become more sustainable. The plastic pollution crisis is going to take not only personal commitment in our households, and not only businesses developing more sustainable solutions, but it will also take electing pro-Earth representatives and passing effective environmental laws.

In my experience, I've found that you don't have to be a politician or even of voting age to create or support legislation. Of course, if you are able to vote in elections, vote for candidates that share your views on the environment. If you are too young to vote, you can volunteer in political campaigns and convince those of voting age—like your parents and grandparents—to vote for your future. You can also raise awareness, so others better understand the issue of plastic pollution. I've found that the more people are educated about something, the better off we all are in this world. So the fifth R alongside *refuse, reduce, reuse,* and *recycle—raise awareness—* simply involves using your personal power to spread knowledge to other citizens and participating in the political process to create widespread awareness.

When I created Plastic Pollution Awareness Day, my aim was to show people that the growing plastics crisis was a bipartisan, global issue. To do so, I paired up with a Republican senator. The next year, I had the same aim, but I worked with a Democratic senator. I wanted to prove that you can work with either political party to achieve results, because plastic pollution isn't a Democratic or Republican issue; it's a global issue, and we need to work together to solve it. I was able to prove that if you use your power of persuasion as a young person, you can be successful working with either political party. Remember: Our political representatives work for *us*, not the other way around. And the ideas for laws that representatives introduce are typically conceived by ordinary people.

Introducing legislation can have a huge and immediate impact on reducing plastic consumption. For instance, the United Kingdom saw more than an

80 percent drop in plastic bag usage by introducing a small fee on plastic bags. Turkey is seeing similar results with their fee on plastic bags. Other countries such as France are banning single-use plastics altogether. The island of Bali has also banned plastic bags, thanks to the leadership of two young sisters.

Melati and Isabel Wijsen, at the ages of ten and twelve, respectively, were inspired by learning about people such as Nelson Mandela and Mahatma Gandhi in school, so they began campaigning against plastic bags in their home of Bali. After the governor repeatedly refused to meet with the sisters, they decided to go on a hunger strike. Within twenty-four hours, they got an opportunity to meet with the governor, and he agreed to ban plastic bags in Bali. Their nonprofit, Bye Bye Plastic Bags, has grown to become an international movement to inspire youth and educate them on plastic bags. It is clear that Bali is better off due to the leadership of these two sisters.

There are several states and cities in the United States—including California, Connecticut, Delaware, Hawaii, Maine, New York, Oregon, and Vermont—

that are also passing laws and making a difference. Honolulu, Hawaii, is one such example, as they have passed a law that phases out single-use plastics. One of my friends, Dyson Chee, was involved in passing this ban. Living in Hawaii, Dyson considers the ocean his second home. As he grew older, he would see more and more plastic threatening the ocean he loved so dearly, but he wasn't sure what he could do to help. I first met him in 2018 when we attended a youth conference called Ocean Heroes Bootcamp, and the conference ignited a fire in him to take action. With his new knowledge and resources, he started Project O.C.E.A.N. Hawaii to fight plastic pollution through education and activism. Despite not being of voting age, he played a role in passing Honolulu's single-use plastic ban. He also did a great job in getting dozens of other concerned citizens to write to Honolulu's city council to express their support. At Dyson's urging, I wrote several letters as a show of support, and I feel good that my little effort might have made a difference.

There is power in numbers. That's the key to influencing businesses and policy, because change really starts with everyday citizens using their voices. As I always say, "Change starts on the ground and it starts with us." More and more people are learning that plastic pollution is a major environmental challenge. Thankfully, it has finally become a mainstream topic in the news and is getting the attention it deserves.

Seven years ago, when I first started talking about plastic pollution, very few people knew about the severity of it or were truly aware of their plastic footprint. But through our collective efforts, and through events like Plastic Pollution Awareness Day, where we exchange and spread knowledge about this crisis, we are beginning to make great strides toward correcting the problem. So the fifth R—*raise awareness*—is very important to fighting plastic pollution.

The simplest act of refusal has some of the most long-term positive impacts on the world. For example, if a family of four eliminates the use of plastic bags over a ten-year time period, that equals approximately twenty thousand plastic bags that are not manufactured, transported, used, and discarded. Now *that's* an impact! Imagine what an entire community can accomplish . . . what entire nations can accomplish . . . what entire generations of concerned citizens can accomplish.

Like Robert Swan warned, the greatest threat to the planet is the belief that someone else will save it. But our greatest strength is our voices. We cannot sit idly while plastic continues to wash up on our beaches, and into animals' mouths and our own bodies. Let all of our voices be heard.

This is our moment. This is our movement. This is our mission.

And it starts now.

ABOUT US

Pocket Change Collective was born out of a need for space. Space to think. Space to connect. Space to be yourself. And this is your invitation to join us.

These books are small, but they are mighty. They ask big questions and propose even bigger solutions. They show us that no matter where we come from or where we're going, we can all take part in changing the communities around us. Because the possibilities of how we can use our space for good are endless.

So thank you. Thank you for picking this book up. Thank you for reading. Thank you for being a part of the Pocket Change Collective.